THE HOLY SIGHT

An Invitation to Holy Relationships…with everyone and everything…

By

Mary Saint-Marie / Sheoekah

ISBN: 1-4140-1891-6 (e-book)
ISBN: 1-4140-1890-8 (Paperback)

This book is printed on acid free paper.

1stBooks - rev. 01/28/04

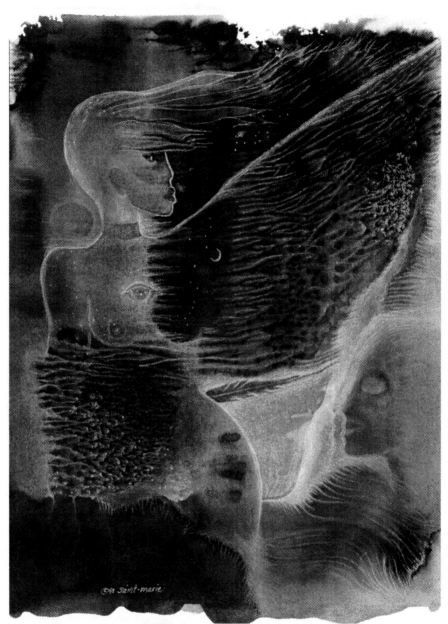

Sky-dancer-SHE © Mary Saint-Marie 1991

This book is dedicated to the Oneness.

And may it serve through inspiration that all may open
to the guidance of the inner and outer teachers who
continue to guide us to the one true inner Teacher.

Acknowledgments

I am in deepest appreciation to the Silence, out of which this book arose, as I traveled about doing art exhibits, sessions and workshops.

I am in such gratitude to my two precious daughters, Kimberly Backes and Rebecca Allen, who love me through my continuing expansion of Consciousness that has unfolded for me a most unusual and unexpected life of much solitude. I thank Michael Backes and Elliot Rawitch and their families who have been so loving and generous with me. I thank the young one, Maya, who comes to me inwardly and continues to help light the way. I thank my dear sister of Light, Laura Daen, who has always 'seen' me and been fully present in her manifested joy with me. I thank my friend, Dixie Lee, who has always been there for me in unconditional caring. I thank my friend, K. Michael Hyatt, who challenges me, inspires me and initiates me in unprecedented ways into spiritual awareness and consciousness.

I thank all the dear ones who have come to me over the years for sessions, retreats, and workshops and continued to insist that I write this book. I really heard you all. When I opened to it, the book was just there.

I thank those at 1st Books Library who have assisted me to give these principles and love a "book body," that I might share with others.

And I am in gratitude to the countless people who helped me with the computer aspects of this endeavor.

Preface

THE HOLY SIGHT is a book about deeply awakening to the awareness of who we really are. It is about awakening to the awareness of the Holy Presence in everyone and everything. It is about humanity's need to see past appearances in the physical universe using Holy Sight to see the transcendence, the Presence that already is, everywhere.

THE HOLY SIGHT is about humanity's urgent need to move beyond unholy sight that would only serve to keep it in fear and bondage, the offspring of separation that causes untold pain and suffering through the eons of rising and falling civilizations.

THE HOLY SIGHT is a book that inspires a shift into a vision of wholeness, into a vision of the garden, that already is. It is a book that inspires a shift from the bondage borne of unholy sight to come into freedom caused by Holy Sight.

Holy Sight is shared as a state of consciousness that can be practiced, experienced and felt. It is a state of consciousness that breaks one out of humanity's spell of unholy sight. That awareness lifts one into the "what is…what already is." Life will change. Divine alchemy rearranges and reorganizes one's life under the sacred and precious gaze of Holy Sight.

Holy Sight is namaste. It goes beyond a momentary greeting. It is a way of seeing…a way of life. This book will lift others into the realization that we can Namaste everything…for Presence is "everywhere present." Practices are included in the book.

THE HOLY SIGHT reveals our individual and collective need for transcendent vision. In this vision, forgiveness happens. The new culture of an awareness of Oneness can only emerge with forgiveness. The book then reveals that divine alchemy unfolds in one's life as this Oneness is known directly. The Law of Balance appears in our lives individually and collectively. The Law of Balance is Love...the Infinite expressed.

This book is a revelation. This is the revelation that has come to me through many inner and outer experiences. I did not have the understanding of how to maintain this state of consciousness, so it has taken me many years of practice. Those years of practice have yielded the gift of serving as a spiritual educator via many forms. I have worked in Soul Sessions and Soul Retreats with large numbers of people from all over the world for over 15 years. This book will serve the continued global awakening.

This book is an initiation.

Mary Saint-Marie

Creating an Exalted Now

Let us create an exalted Now through the Art of Holy Sight.
Let us enact this internal alchemy in our lives.
Let us discover it is a law of the Universe.
Let us discover, that through practice, one returns from the finite
sense of things in the ever human mind of concept and judgment, lost
in separation from Spirit, to the Energy of the Universe... Love...
Essence... Revelation... Beauty... Balance...

Holy Sight allows a return to Oneness in Consciousness.
It allows a grand remembering of the One Soul.
It allows one to be animated spontaneously by Spirit.

When we engage in Holy Sight, we see the wholeness of another...the
divine in another...the true identity of another. When that mystical
moment happens, there is no need to forgive. It has already
happened, as we are willing to see the person beyond human
appearance and see the truth of another.

Holy Sight...is Namaste...
Holy Sight...is Beauty lived...
Holy Sight...is a journey of Grace...revealed...

Together...let us go upon this journey...

Cover art poem by Mary Saint-Marie:

Behold-SHE

SHE does sit among the stars...
and SHE...does see the world...
The world...SHE knows...
doth dwell within...

It mirrors forth...and lo...
Creation does seem to lie...
before our very eyes...

This painting reveals that the world lies within our
Consciousness...and it is an invitation to find that
place where all are One...

This painting is of a masked-SHE...under which
is this precious Universe...
Behold...

Passages of The Holy Sight

"Invitation to Holy Relationships" with everyone and everything...

The Holy Sight is an ancient practice, known by the illumined. It educates about a very simple practice. It is so simple as to be easily missed and/or ignored. It has been deeply misunderstood and/or ignored by not only the Western Mind, but most of the world in the constant rising and falling of civilizations and nations throughout history, in the avid practice of "unholy sight."

"Unholy sight" is not an easy habit to change. There are centuries of belief in "unholy sight." It has become socially acceptable. It is considered to be clear perception of the world outside of us that has gone astray. Truly, it is being under the "spell of the seeming appearance world." It takes understanding, then practice, to break that spell, that our lives, then the world might change.

Worlds of institutionalized opinions of human good and bad in various cultures, traditions, and civilizations carefully guard and protect these deeply entrenched social beliefs that allow and even applaud at times "unholy sight."

One has to be willing to look at history and honestly see that these concepts and beliefs have not worked and do not work. They manage and contain. They inhibit and control. They do not effect an authentic transformation from within. They do not provide a context for a collective shift of consciousness. They do not penetrate the appearance world of time and space. They do not provide a foundation for a culture of love. They miss the point of life. They are thoughts borne of separation from the One Life.

We can break the collective spell. We can engender change from the inside out, one person by one person. This change can only occur in consciousness. And only a change in consciousness can effect an authentic change in the seeming outer world.

It must be first understood that there is only consciousness. Consciousness unfolding. When that is deeply understood, the inspiration to shift awareness comes on its own...and change...it does come. This inner shift...creates an outer shift. It is the way of the universe. Let us align with this knowing...and allow the mystery to unfold.

What is it...that can shift our mind and the Western Mind...and all minds in all its relationships...with everyone and everything?

What is it...that can turn belief from material sense and outer appearance?

What is it...that can break the spell that is the "outer seeming" of the world of fear, pain and suffering borne of separation from Source?

What is it...that can allow deep forgiveness...easily...naturally?

I say...

Let us...come into Holy Sight...
Let us...see the Truth of Being...
Let us...see the Wholeness...that Already Is...
Let us...see that I Am Everywhere...
Let us...feel this Holy Presence...as everywhere Present...

I say...let us together midwife the birth into Oneness Consciousness, that the global "practice of malpractice," that is, seeing one another in our humanness, can be shifted...and the "spell of seeming separation" be broken. In no way, does this condone or accept or agree with harmful behavior. It only describes a shift of awareness, of consciousness, for self and others that allows a universal alchemy. It allows a rearranging and restructuring of that which we see as our physical and 3-D existence. It allows the quantum physics understanding of subjective beliefs as affecting the experiment...of beliefs as affecting the experiment. Those beliefs penetrate and infuse and create our very world. It allows us to enter an adventure of Life rarely imagined by the human mind, so plagued and diseased it is with these opinions and judgments of the "appearance" world.

These concepts and beliefs are understandable. Clearly. They are the logical and reasonable opinions to adopt. They "seem" so true. Rather obvious, like "seeing is believing." One day we shall see that "believing is seeing" and that we have often ignorantly, innocently and inadvertently misused this amazing mind, just waiting to be filled with illumined and Holy Sight.

This practice of Holy Sight may be used easily by people of any religion, tradition, background or profession. It is a power filled awareness that can radically shift any relationship. It can turn around man/woman relationships, family relationships, corporate and legal relationships, and friend and colleague relationships.

Most important, it may shift "enemy" relationships. It carries the power of the Infinite. It can part the Red Sea. It is a higher Alchemy when really understood. It has the Power of the sweetest global unification. It is profound in the possibilities. Books could be written just on the possibilities. The mind just has not entertained the world from this perspective.

This shift is a "shift of awareness" that can be experienced, practiced and lived. And our life changes. No one need even know you are doing it. And change...it happens anyway. It is then that the Mystical is known as the Practical. It can be appreciated as the "as above, so below." It can be appreciated as the "as within, so without." It can be appreciated as a scientific law or principle that works in our world. This shift of consciousness may transfigure the mind and effects may even be felt in our physical body. It is often felt as a rush of Energy that returns to us when the mind is no longer blocking it with a false concept. It may actually shift the molecules in our world. It seems that I speak of miracles. It is not a miracle. It is simple. It is ordinary. It is normal. And yet it is the paradox, for it is simultaneously extraordinary, paranormal and seemingly miraculous.

We must find the place where the paradox happens. It is the sacred journey. And it is ours to find.

It is little known. The "world is within." It looks so simple. The world seems to be outside of us. It is not. It is within. Our

3

consciousness, as our cherished beliefs and concepts, are creating, attracting, ruling and often destroying our world. And we then are feeling the victim and the receiver of bad fortune.

In 1981, in deep meditation, I had a mystical/practical nine hour revelation that the "world is within." (In truth, there was no one left to have Holy Sight. There was only pure Awareness. There was simply Consciousness. It was outside the realm of teachers and teachings, for there was only knowing. Direct knowing. I was not aware of myself as a knower.) This glimpse into reality did not keep me from falling back under part of the spell of separation from Source, for I did not know how to maintain and sustain such an expanded state of awareness of Being. And I was still so entrenched in my own human habits of belief and living.

This chasm that now existed in me between the mystical/practical awareness of being and the old learned belief structures that dwelled in my ever human mind, quite content to "see the appearance as true," began to create a struggle in my consciousness. I knew the one which was true, yet I did not have an understanding of the profound principles that would allow a new world to emerge. I birthed at that time great compassion for the predicament of the "seeming world." And I began a new journey.

If we do not understand these principles, this may all sound ludicrous, even stupid, to the human mind. For the human mind cannot even travel to the consciousness of which I speak. It may not even peek or glimpse this Consciousness. It is outside the ever human mind filled with all its opinions of good and bad. It is a Oneness Mind that illumines "What Is" for each of us.

What follows in this book is an "Invitation to Holy Relationships" with everyone and everything. This is attained through conscious awareness of the Current of Life. It is attained with Holy Sight. It does not matter what names we give this Current of Life. We may give it generic names, religious names, traditional names, metaphysical names or our own special names. We may call it Infinite, Source, Holy Spirit, Universal Soul, Energy, Chi, Governing

Force, Oneness, Christ Mind, Om, the Mother of the World, Great Spirit, Great Mystery, Buddha Mind, Mother/Father God, etc.

It does not matter. When we open to this Holy Presence, we go beyond to that which is paradoxically wordless and nameless, to that which is timeless.

When we merge with this Current of Life, our Life begins to change. The Holy Sight allows us to feel and know this Presence...everywhere. This Power of Awareness...allows the renewal of the mind. It allows the transfiguration of the ever human mind. It allows the human mind to become a transparency for the One Mind. It allows a Oneness Consciousness to be glimpsed. It allows one to have revelations of oneness with everyone and everything. It allows the initial revelations that interconnectedness Is, that interrelatedness Is. These are not theories or philosophical pursuits. These are not scientific postulates. They are simply...very simply...What Is!

This "What Is" awaits the knowing of humanity. We must awaken to the fact that we are 'the living revelation.' No one can give it to us. No one can do it for us. No one can buy it or sell it. It is a solitary journey. It is our birthright. It is our heritage. It is who we are. It is our unfolding awareness. It seems to play hide and seek with us...and we do not see.

Others may initiate us, catalyze us, reinspire us, touch us, move us. We do the practice. This is a world where ultimately we drop all sense of mediums and intercessors. This is a direct journey.

We must see...first individually and then one by one... moving into the "collective knowing." It spreads...for it is "What Is." When no more attention is on the miscreations of human duality, the battle of good and bad, another world may emerge. New homes, villages, cities, nations and cultures may emerge. New lives may emerge.

We begin to see that it is a simple understanding. The "living" of it is the opportunity to grow and shift and change and to be a part of this emerging world...out of the ashes of the old. It is the phoenix rising, first in individual consciousness and into collective consciousness.

We cannot delegate and demand and war for change. Even peace treaties have proven not to work. Pushing around the physical world with mental and physical force has already historically proven itself fruitless and futile. It is a struggle with no end. It is a battle with no end. It feeds upon itself and consumes all who fall prey to the social belief in disorder.

It is difficult to believe, but we live in a spiritual universe. Order Is. Peace Is. Love Is. It can only be found with Holy Sight. We are in the greatest transformation the world has ever known.

> In the aerial, global picture,
> this simple shift of consciousness
> to Holy Sight may allow the
> movement from warring civilizations
> to the creation of cultures borne of Love...
> borne of the simple dance of the One...

We ask why have we not known this?
Why have we not been told?

We must ask. We must ask to know.
We must open to know. We must desire to know...

And knowing comes. The Mystery...She unveils herself.
She stands naked and She dances...

Let us begin...

It is not necessary to have degrees or an intellectual or scientific mind to begin this practice. It is simple. A child may do it. Come into child-like wonder. Come into wonder. The wonder...opens to the mystery of "What Is."

Come...let us begin...

"What Is" cannot be found via mediums and intercessors. "What Is" is found through an open and transparent mind, allowing "Presence" to reveal itself. It is not only a "knowing." It is a direct knowing. And through it our world changes. It is a holy act.

We have been told many times, by many Messengers, via many teachings, that "What Is" cannot be found on a holy mountain, or a holy temple or in a holy book. It can only be found within. Those places, buildings or books may catalyze or provide a conducive environment. Yet the kingdom is within. The world is within.

Let us begin this day to see "what is."

We have been told to become as a child. It does not take academic training to become a child. It takes a consciousness that will look through the outer appearance and see the true identity of the soul that is really there before us. It takes a great willingness to break the spell of the "outer appearance." And we must go beyond our idolizing of the spiritual messengers. They never asked us to do that. They had a message. In that message is our "freedom." Go within. The withiness is this Holy Nameless Presence. And in that withiness, we begin to glimpse another world. Then, it is, that Holy Sight is possible. We must not lose the living of the message by getting caught up in the life of the messenger.

The Holy Sight...for Self...

The Holy Sight is not an intellectual endeavor. Nor is it information to fill the human mind. Nor is it even something to discuss, argue or debate. It is an awareness. It is a simple awareness, caused by a shift in consciousness. Only then can its gift be given. Only then can its gift be realized, actualized and experienced. Only then can its luminous alchemy become one's very life.

The Holy Sight is a portal, an opening, a doorway, a passage. And it is an initiation into a new life. One's life as it has been lived cannot stay the same as one inhabits the practice. The practice is the awareness of Holy Sight.

There are many portals. This portal is powerful because it causes sight and insight of the Real and it dissolves and erases false beliefs that are ages and even eons old.

The rich tapestry of an illumined humanity lies just beneath "old concepts, opinions and judgments of good and bad." Beyond this mental and social morality lies a world of IS. It IS filled already with harmony, with peace and with all the other qualities and attributes of God, the Nameless One. These qualities and attributes are far from personal. We cannot even acquire them though the opposite seems so. We are that. We are Already that. Just beneath the layer/layers of concepts...illumination IS.

And through that portal, there is no separation. There is no fear. There is no longer even a portal. There is just pure Awareness. Awareness IS. I Am.

It is much more simple to have Holy Sight for others if we can come deeply into the Holy Sight for ourselves. The false beliefs we have about who we are block us from the awareness of Holy Presence. We are locked unknowingly in the prison of our own thoughts about our body, mind, emotions...our past, present, future and all our relationships.

The following meditation opens the mental prison doors. We are free. It is the true freedom. People and nations of the world search everywhere for "freedom from." Freedom from abuses, enemies, negativities, mental and emotional assaults. Freedom from cruelty, slavery, control. Freedom from endless forms of unkindness. Freedom from fear. We can achieve that. Only to find that another prison has arrived. We must shift from "freedom from" to "freedom in"... "freedom in Presence."

A few years ago, I was returning to America from a trip to Brazil. I was reading one of the airline magazines. In it was one of the most beautiful stories of Holy Sight that I have ever heard. A man had begun going to a prison in his area on the weekends. He was able to meet with those who were open to his message. He began sharing with prisoners who were open. He told them that beneath their beliefs about being bad and evil people, that they were one with the Infinite. He told them that their problems were caused by their identification with badness. Some of the inmates began to listen. He began to teach them how to meditate on this totally unknown Infinite. One day, one of the men who was in prison for life, had an experience beyond the human mind. He saw himself with Holy Sight. He was now out of his own mental prison. Somehow he was pardoned and released from prison. He went through school and became a minister, that he could serve others. This man truly caught the message of The Holy Sight. It became his life and his gift. It became the blessing of our social order.

Freedom in Presence...allows another life. Life borne of exultation is possible. I am not speaking of a life known by monks, sages and saints locked away in caves or mountains or monasteries. We are those monks, sages and saints. We are That. There is no need to shut out life. Embrace life. Allow life. Allow Presence to inhabit you. Freedom is.

Freedom from bad is part of the struggle of humanity caught in the fascinating battle of duality, good and evil, light and dark, the white and black hats. Truly, now, there is "another world."

10

Let us begin…

Meditation 1

This meditation may be done alone or with the guidance of an attuned one.
Take each sentence very slowly, with gaps of time between to feel the experience.
We will slowly come into a deepening.

First close your eyes gently. Become aware of your breath. Get comfortable in your sitting space. Move around a bit until you feel very comfortable. Feeling is very important and is a key into this Journey into Oneness. It is the feminine expression of our Beingness, without which, we live aimlessly in the world of mind, that is words and thoughts, concepts and beliefs. Let us use feeling this day as a portal to transcend the human mind. Be aware of and feel this Presence of God, this Oneness of Creator as Creation. The 'as above, so below' is not two. It is One.

Begin now to be aware of your breathing. Breathe slowly and gently and at your own intuited rhythm and pace. Again the key is to feel, that we may recover our receptive, our yin and feminine aspect. Then we may awaken to the Presence of God, with direct knowing, with no mediums or intercessors of any kind. Our developed ability to be receptive is our ability to surrender and to relax into this awareness of Presence.

Continue to put your attention on breath, your inhalations and your exhalations, as I share a story that most of us have heard. It is a profound story if heard with inner hearing. And it can change our lives. It is the story of *Aladdin and the Lamp.* We all remember that Aladdin has a magic lamp which he rubs. Out comes the mysterious genie in a burst of smokey mist to grant his wish. Friends, we are that Aladdin lamp, genie and wish. And how we rub the lamp is with our Awareness. Awareness of the Holy Presence. That is the power of Awareness. It sounds so simple. However, the outer world distracts us in many ways. And only we can bring our attention back to this Holy Presence through awareness and feeling.

Through this portal of awareness, you may come into Holy Presence. This Presence is omnipresent. That is, it is everywhere present. Presence IS. And it is in and through all form in the visible and nonvisible worlds. Presence IS.

We may call this Presence by other names, such as Light, Source, Power, Consciousness, Divine, Zero of Stillness, God, Father, Mother, Allah, Great Spirit, Life, Force and Love, yet truly this is the Nameless One, for It transcends all words. It transcends all time and space, yet paradoxically, it fills it all. Omnipresent...an all-present isness...beingness. Ultimately, it is more something to be lived and experienced than to be named and discussed.

Become aware more deeply of your breathing. Inhale. Exhale. Breathe slowly. Continue awareness around the breath as we continue.

Now become aware of the visible world of form...the visible world as you know it. Honor it through your awareness. This thankfulness, this appreciation, has a powerful effect of bringing the 'feeling' of inner communion. Thankfulness is extremely powerful. For gratitude is a law of the universe. Now become aware of your own visible body form. And be aware of forms everywhere. Again be honoring...and feel your gratitude. Feeling is a key. It is a gift of the feminine principle.

Next become aware of the invisible world of form. It has thought forms, energy forms, image forms and even discarnate entity forms. And the quantum physicists have informed us that we can even stare into space to a particular spot and a particle will form where none existed. All is in Consciousness before manifestation on the physical level. Again, feel gratitude for this invisible world of form. Feeling will continue to be a powerful agent and gift. It is a key.

Stretch now your consciousness, your awareness to that which is both invisible and formless. That is Holy Presence. It is formless, timeless, wordless and nameless, while paradoxically it is everywhere present.

Simultaneously, stay aware of your breathing. From this realm of Presence, take a slow deep inhalation allowing it to enter every cell of your body. Envision each cell as a beautiful open lotus flower, the petals fully open to receive this Light, this Presence that is the invisible formless realm. As this Presence enters all your cells in every part of your body, 'feel' that Presence. Feel it everywhere. And know that though we are using visualization to bring your awareness to the Presence of Light, be aware that we are doing this to shift your awareness from human body awareness and identity to Light awareness and identification as that Light. The truth is that you are already this Light.

Remember the power of awareness. Your awareness begins to make it real and happening in your seemingly personal world. Awareness activates this Light in your world. Your awareness is the catalyst. You become your own initiator by bringing your awareness to Presence of Light. Your outer life then begins to change…via your inner consciousness. The ancient passage, 'as above, so below," begins to occur in your life. Above and below are now experienced as One, with no separation. An inspired life from Presence is lived rather than a life motivated by the human mind and all its fears and imaginings. All inwardly inspired life is perfection.

Take one more slow and deep breath, from the realm of Presence, in through all the lotus petals that are your cells, bathing all your cells in Light. Now just feel the Light that you already are, always have been and always will be.

Repeat that inhalation. This time bring your awareness of the incoming Light into your heart. Begin to slowly and softly breathe into and from your heart center. Feel the warmth of the Presence of Light now in your heart. Be aware that that Presence is Love and that Love is who you are. That Love is who you already are. That is the Light manifest in this 3-D world as you. The Light manifest as you. Remember the passage from scripture, 'I and the Father are One,' not two, but one, in union. The lover and the beloved as one. The Mystical Marriage exists within our Consciousness. Feel that Light. Merge with that Light. Identify with that Light.

Take a moment now and visualize yourself as two inches high in your heart. See yourself as a glowing and brilliant light, a divine child of light. It does not matter what age you picture yourself for you are ageless. Use whatever image comes to you and feels right. Trust yourself. For there is only one Self. And it is the Divine Self. Use your power of awareness to know this as your true self, your true beingness that is fully whole and complete. It has never been spoiled, tainted, hurt or diseased. It has never birthed and never died. It knows no limits.

On your next exhale, begin to allow this 2 inch high self of light to grow and expand spherically like a glowing and radiating sun. Feel it. Feel it as it fills all the atoms and molecules of your body. Allow yourself to be bathed in this radiation of Light. Feel this Light.

As this light of yourself radiates outwardly from your heart, allow it to move on through your skin, realizing you are an energy body. Allow it to continue on out into your auric field. See your energy field extend out around your body, about three feet in all directions. Allow yourself to feel the love that is this luminous egg emanating from you. Continue to keep your awareness on feeling this Presence of Light that you already are.

Be aware that much of humanity still believes that it is a body. Humanity still strongly identifies with its body, its thoughts, its emotions, and careers and roles and spouses. Because of this we have endless cases of mistaken identity. For we are Consciousness. We are one with the Light. We must identify with the Light of Knowing.

As you continue to breathe, use your awareness to begin to merge with this Light. Be one with this Light. Become transparent for this Light. Be aware of the inner union of the lover and the beloved. This is the Mystical and Holy Marriage, the alabaster wedding. Feel this union with Light, this Oneness.

And again be aware that this Light is everywhere present, Omnipresent. It centers us from the seeming outside and inside with every inhalation and exhalation. Without breath, we leave this form.

14

So again take a deep slow inhalation from the invisible formless realm of the Infinite Presence into the heart. As you begin to exhale, allow your inhalation and exhalation to merge, using that merge as a portal to go even deeper into the Stillness and Silence of the One.

Now just Be.
Just Be in the awareness of this Presence…
Feel…Presence IS…
Stay deeply with this awareness…
Holy Presence…IS…
As you continue to practice, you will develop the spiritual consciousness that allows the awareness to arise softly and gently with only those two words…
Presence…IS…
It is a state of consciousness attained…

Meditation 2

Desire the Presence of God. Desire to be alone in this Presence. Be aware that as you concentrate on this desire of Presence that you will next find yourself beginning to decentrate. It will begin to feel as if the outer world is falling away. You will begin to notice distractions and concerns falling away. Be aware of moving inwardly into the Silence…into the Stillness…into what seems to be the void, a sanctuary of withinness.

Be aware that your identity with your body begins to dissolve. Be aware that your concentration on God keeps other thoughts from coming in. Notice that you relax.

Notice that an inner joy arises. If you go ever deeper, you will be aware of rapture.

Allow your self to be aware of pure Consciousness. Be aware of this Light of Knowing as your very self.

If you have a question, a problem, a concern, put that in this Light of Knowing. There is nothing that we cannot know. Know yourself as Consciousness. Know yourself as Light. The greatest teacher is the Teacher Within.

Extending Holy Sight to others

It is this Holy Sight for our self that is so important. When we have learned to have this Holy Sight, as an experience, for ourselves, then we can learn to extend this Love to others, that is, we can share Holy Sight with all those who cross our path on what we call our Life. Holy Sight for self and other selves is a profound initiation that does change our lives. The world does respond. Our life does change.

When we extend Holy Sight to others, we are extending love...balance to others. When we can feel and know this Presence within ourselves, we are then able to be aware of that same Presence in others. If you are having a difficult time with anyone, just sit down in meditation and find that place of wholeness within yourself. Then see the other person in front of you. Begin to see them also breathe in the Light of Presence. Be aware of them inhaling this Light and exhaling this Light. You may have a myriad of emotional or negative thoughts come up; allow them to surface, but do not entertain or indulge them. Continue to feel the Presence of your own being and then simultaneously be aware of the other person as this Light manifest. Stay with this knowing until you feel the energy shift of your own revelation of their true identity as Light. Then you will know that you have extended Holy Sight.

Holy Sight and Presence

We are not able to practice Holy Sight unless we have the ability to experience this Presence, this Holy Presence. This Presence is everywhere present, that is, it is omnipresent. This experience allows us to grow in great compassion and limitless love.

Then, it is, that arises from our Soul, is the openness to "feel" Presence everywhere. Then, it is, that we grow and expand in our sense of aliveness, our sense of connectedness and in our sense of relatedness. Then, it is, that we begin to have experiences of belonging. We belong to this life we are in. We may "feel" a Oneness with the minerals, the plants, the animals and all of humanity. We may "feel" a Oneness with the air, earth, water, metal and fire. These kingdoms and elements are sacred. They are the expressions of Presence in endless forms.

Until we align with and feel this Presence, we experience the sense of separateness, out of which is borne fear and its offsprings of pain, suffering and misery.

First individually, then collectively, let us expand our awareness of Presence.
Presence IS...
Presence IS everywhere...
Be aware of it...
Feel it...
Allow it to animate your body and your mind...

It is both wisdom and love.
It is the age old Law of Balance.
And it awaits our knowing.
With knowing...is borne the actions.
Actions borne of the Law of Balance are the healing balm sought for by humanity.

All of the movies looking for the Holy Grail and the Arc of the Holy Covenant are beautiful and fascinating in that they awaken the viewer to the remembering of a Something bigger, Something greater than the human mind. That Something is a Holy Presence that can be found within. It is a state of Consciousness.

It will not be found in the never ending outer odysseys to the end of the world. It will be found in the heart and soul of our being. It will be found at the end of the external travel...when the journey turns inward. There...it will be found.

We can search endlessly in corridors of time and space. It will not be found.

It is timeless.

Together...let us enter into this Timeless Realm and let us find that we are One. The human mind will never comprehend this. So we must leave the human mind. It is not our guide; rather it is the exquisite instrument through which Mind, the One Mind, can speak, when we have ceased our fascination with concepts, theories, beliefs, opinions of good and bad. When also our fascination with pathology ceases, we can allow life to pour through us, as us. We can behold life everywhere. Life begins to be experienced as an illumined holographic mandala.

And time...it ceases...

Humanity is about to begin a new life borne of this Timeless Presence. Individually, we can begin it now. The more individuals there are, that are living in this state of consciousness, the faster will be the transition for the collective. For we soon discover...there is nothing but Consciousness.

That collective discovery, will trigger great amends. Forthcoming will be grand celebrations of global forgiveness. The celebrations will bring even nations together. An ethnic appreciation will be borne that is beyond comprehension. No longer will there be focus on war but focus on the joy of multiplicity of expression of the Infinite.

Astonishment does not even begin to describe what will transpire as great numbers awaken out from under humanity's collective spell of separateness.

This call to Oneness is being heard by many sensitive souls. Soon it shall be felt by many more. They are even now becoming dissatisfied with the habits and practices that keep one in the spell of a world in fear and pain, borne of seeming separation.

Celebration awaits the collective.
Celebration awaits the awakening ones.
Celebration is Life itself... for those who live in Presence Now.
Come...let us celebrate.

Come...let us understand that in Presence is Holy Sight.

Holy Sight and the Present Moment

Practicing Holy Sight is a very potent way to stay in the present moment. It demands your awareness to be fully conscious of "Presence Is." Presence Already Is. Not tomorrow. Not yesterday. This moment. Now.

Now is the time to practice Holy Sight. Now is the time to use the precious scenario in front of you to practice. The scene before you is an opportunity and it carries a gift.

As you practice Holy Sight, you automatically practice Presence. With everyone you see, another opportunity arises to look past appearance and outer seeming and to penetrate the illusion to see "what is." To see "what already is."

Each moment is a precious moment for this awareness. It is not easy always for the mind to give up what seems to be concrete evidence in the material world.

But the rewards are there for those who practice Holy Sight. The rewards are not what we are used to. They can come in many ways. Energy may return to us. A feeling of upliftment may come. A feeling of inner joy may arise. A smile may form upon our lips. Weight may leave the shoulders, leaving relaxed muscles. A feeling of peace that cannot be given by the world may come. A knowing that all is well, even if the evidence is contrary to that, may be felt. The heart may open. Even an otherworldly overshadowing of grace may come.

Relationships change. Doors open. A new world…it does emerge.

What grace does follow Holy Sight…

Entire histories shall change as Holy Sight becomes the vision of the day. Entire civilizations may emerge from beneath the rubble of a sight borne of hatred. History may even fall away, discarded as unneeded baggage. People with clear sight will create only Beauty. For through them, only Beauty can be seen.

O, we sit at heaven's doors and know it not. Sometimes we see humanity pounding and screaming and even praying at heaven's door…to "let me in." And one day we find…the door was never shut. The closed door is imagined in the mind full of beliefs and concepts. The door was never shut. There was never even a door.

> My friends…I say…
> only Presence is…

Let us not broadcast this from mountain tops.
Let us wear this in a robe of silence.
Let us practice.
And we need say nothing…
ever…

Life becomes easy, for Holy Sight brings recognition and realization that "Presence is."

Joy arises in the heart for each meeting, for each path crossed, for each thought of one's ever dwelling in our mind. Joy becomes the news of the day. For "Presence is;" there is no other.

We may have a hard day or days or even weeks. We may meet some problems. But we can know, from our own experience, that it is created by the mind. Problems arise in the mind. And we may go beyond the mind. We may rise above the realm of problems.
We may leave that world behind.

And we will find that we live in another world, while yet in this world. For a while we may go back and forth. There are always friends, family and acquaintances…even strangers on the street ready to invite us back into the world of problems.

It is a make-believe world. It is not true. We are under the spell of the belief that we must live with problems.

What joy does await our seeing.

When one whines and says, "I can't," then that is so. "I can't" does create a mental block, a barrier that is stronger than steel. Be ever alert of the thoughts we decide to believe. They could block our inherent joy.
They could keep us from heaven's door.
They could give us the excuses that we are looking for.

The awareness of "I can" does remove the barrier. Practice does bring the experience and the direct knowing. And no one can do it for us. Nor can we buy or sell it.

After that, we need no teacher or spiritual messenger to tell us. We need only practice. This is a practice of Love. Holy Sight is a practice of unconditional Love. It does break all barriers, all animosities, all old grudges, ancient family and racial hatreds. Restored is the "lost years of the locust."

New ways of relating begin to come forth.
Love finds unprecedented expression.
North meets South and East meets West.
That which has no direction is thus perceived.
The family of humanity unites.

And night does turn to day...
and day does meet the night...
and love is borne...

Beholding

Holy Sight is a beholding, a witnessing, a seeing of Presence. Become a beholder of Presence…everywhere.

Go into nature, sitting beside a stream or a river, in and among the rocks. Behold Presence in the moving river. Behold Presence in the flying insects, the fish, the birds, the pilots flying overhead. Behold Presence even in the rocks. Behold this Life in the trees, the tiniest wildflowers, the clouds moving across the sky.

Breathe with them. Feel your breath. Feel their breath. Breathe together. Feel the One Breath. Be aware of the Presence of Light radiating from you. Be aware of the Presence of Light radiating from them. Then experience the Light radiating from you touch and merge with the Light radiating from them. The key is to feel. Feel this merge.
Feel this Oneness. There is but one Light. Experience this Light. It is the One. It is Presence. It is the Essence that pervades all form. It is you and it is me. It is the kingdoms and the elements and it is everywhere present.
Everywhere. Feel it everywhere.

Begin to realize this Presence as a Current. It runs through all Life, as all Life. It is Life. And there is but One Life.

When we behold this Presence in our own heart, soul, body and mind, we can begin more easily to behold it everywhere. We realize that we are a part of this vast Current. At night, we behold it as it moves the endless stars across the darkest sky. We behold it bring another dusk and dawn and another drop of rain.

Behold it as ever present and watch your life begin to change. Be attuned with this sacred song…that is life…singing in the heavens and on the earth.

Go into your village or city. Behold Presence in everyone you see. Everyone. As you drive along your roads, behold Presence as the driver of every car. Behold Presence animated even as the homeless. Watch your mind struggle to return to human and social sense of good and bad. Resist the temptation to go into that world that creates fear, pain and suffering. Resist the temptation to react to the world's conditions. Rather than react to the outer world, one begins to respond to Presence and one finds oneself animated by this current…this force…this life…

Behold Presence.

As we watch the outer world, we can easily come under the spell of the human mind's conclusions. The human mind does dwell in concepts of good and bad. And those concepts are ever changing.
Let us lift our awareness into Presence…
Let us find another world…
Let us find a spiritual universe…that ever was…and ever will be…

It is…
Let us Behold…

Notice that peace arises. Not from trying to calm the outer turbulence of the world, but by beholding Presence. Peace cannot be won with treaties and wars and manipulation. Peace is not even won.

Peace is. It already is. Be a one who beholds peace as it unveils itself within your heart and soul. Watch your mind as it begins its new journey of translating and interpreting the language borne of beholding.

Let us find this language of peace that ever dwells within, awaiting the dissolution of the collective spell. Beholding Presence will begin to break open the collective spell.

When my oldest daughter was an infant, I would move her blanket around the living room as the day unfolded, so her eyes would behold the beauty of the shadows of plants in the room as they danced upon the wall and as the sun did move across the sky. I did not know the word Presence then. I simply deeply felt the essence of beauty in flight across the walls and I shared it with the eyes of an infant.

Behold beauty together. Behold Presence together. Find ways, unique ways to behold in every moment.

Beholding is not a technique or a process. Beholding is a way of seeing. It is a way of life, an expanding awareness that nurtures.

Beholding happens now. We cannot escape in our minds into past and future. Beholding keeps our awareness on "what is."

Holy Sight Transports

For many years of individual and group work, ones have said to me, "Holy Sight is very difficult. I do not know if I can see certain people in that way." We each have to decide for ourselves if this is our time to leave the human world of blame, guilt, shame and projection. We have to decide if we will leave the world that would judge one another. We have to decide if we will leave the world that sees the "outer mask of seeming" and believes in that and acts on that. Should we choose to relate to the outer mask, we ourselves will stay in the pain and suffering borne of that malpractice. We shall stay in the bondage of our own thoughts. We shall stay in the prison of our own beliefs and concepts. We think we are comfortable there, for the mind has analyzed the person and/or situation and sees itself as quite perceptive. The mind shouts loudly that it is right.

And we close the doors of that person, we are judging, from changing in relation to us. We ourselves have closed that door. One can see this often in a child who grows up, moves away, and then in going back home a new person, finds that the parents still see him/her in the same way and refuse to see the change, the growth, the difference.

We shall rejoice the day that we see that those thoughts of another's mask keeps us in bondage.

It is ourselves that we are freeing, not the other person. The other person is already the Infinite, whether they have yet realized it or not.

So to the words, "practicing Holy Sight is difficult," I would say this. It is not as difficult as practicing unholy sight, which takes us individually and collectively down a road of hell and a history of hell.

It can take practice to change and shift our way of seeing, but with earnestness and sincerity, it is done. At moments, it may seem a challenge, when the mask shown is horrifying to our eyes. The example of a monster mask on an innocent child at Halloween comes to mind. Life is much like that. The person is acting out their beliefs and underneath that seeming monster, is a hallowed being.

It is then that we have the opportunity to go deeper than the mask. It is then that we have the opportunity to experience transcendent vision and be transported into a life unimagined by a mind dwelling in human good and bad. It is then that we may sanctify our sight. We have the opportunity each moment to go within, feel Presence and then know…Presence IS…everywhere.

At that moment, we have gone beyond the outer appearance, the outer seeming. In that moment, what appears to be magic, is a possibility. If the other person is open, a healing may appear outwardly. For wholeness exists. It already IS.

In our homes, villages, cities and nations, we have ample opportunity to practice. We may practice each day that we hear the seeming bad news blaring in words or sound from the media, neighbors or so called enemies. We can practice as we walk down any street or as we shop in any store. Presence IS! And we shift. Joy arises in our heart and in our soul. As we drive down our local streets or on any major freeways, we can practice.   In Passage 10, I speak of a longer experience of using Holy Sight on the roads. Each time we are on the road, we may have these elevated experiences, if we can remember to stay in Presence. I have had many experiences of feeling the Oneness with all the drivers on a crowded freeway. One feels almost to be floating through a dream experience, yet it is fully grounded and moving in high speed. It is an ecstasy that reveals another world.
It reveals that there is a time in humanity's unfolding that there will no longer be collisions. When we stay conscious and aware and in Presence, there is no longer a possibility that there be collisions. Love unifies. It does not collide and kill.
Let us awaken, each of us, to that much love.   And let us be compassionate when that much awareness is not there. Let us have compassion for ourselves and for others.

As we drive down local streets or on any major freeways, we can practice. We can actually "defuse road rage," in our own lives and behold the highways in our own lives begin to change. Yes, it is difficult. It is only difficult because we have not been educated about this universal principle. We have not been schooled in the laws of the universe. We have not been schooled in the awareness of Presence IS in such a practical usage as driving down the street.

Now is the time. We can accept this as an adventure and begin now. We can each find creative ways to do this. We can turn it into the life-giving part of our day. For it is that...life-giving.

We can find that each time we have Holy Sight, an energy begins to be felt. At first, it may be missed or not noticed, or it might be a tiny tingling feeling in the spine or in the arms. But as you stay sensitive and very aware, each time that you practice Holy Sight, you will discover an energy, no matter how subtle, seems to return to you. Your human thought, borne of separation, borne of duality, borne of judgment, has dissolved and returned to you as what it really is...Love...unconditional Love. That is your energy returned to transport you to a spiritual consciousness.

Here and there we have many small or large moments of rapture when we live in Holy Sight. We are not transported somewhere. We are still in this world, but no longer are we at the horrendous effect of our own unholy sight. We have moments of freedom in this newly found Presence. This is freedom in Presence. And truly, we feel transported in consciousness.

Inner Presence begins to register in our minds and outpictures as our outer world. We see that there is no separation. We see that it was all the time in the human mind that loves the play of opposites.

The world is within...
Another world begins...
Let us smile...

Mystic Marriage

We cannot enter the Mystic Marriage within if we entertain unholy sight for others. This unholy sight does create mental blocks. This unholy sight does consist of our finite and human concepts, beliefs, opinions and judgments. How we can feel so righteous about our unholy sight is because the finite sense of things is so strong. We are so under the spell of the lie that we fully believe it is true.

Holy Sight may assist to bring us out from under the spell, that we may enter unto the Mystic Marriage. The Mystic Marriage is conscious union with Presence within and sense of separation ceases.
It is the Oneness with the illumined tapestry of creation.
It is the long talked about interconnectedness and relatedness.
It is the living experience.
It is that which reveals direct that we are all brothers and sisters.
It is an unblemished purity.
It is sweet…
It is sacred…
It is wholeness revealed as an illumined holographic mandala…of Mind…
The One Mind…
It rules…
There is no exception…

Concept to the contrary is illusion and deception. It is a lie and a spell. And it has the ability to hypnotize. All the offspring of fear, which are pain, suffering and misery in endless forms, are signposts that we have made a mistake in our mind. To clear and renew the mind, we need to give it new thoughts. As the mind entertains and dwells in new and holy ideas of wholeness, it is inspired to move into a new role of receiving awareness of Presence. It can be in the silence…sublime and placid…reflecting the Infinite.

Then…it is…
the Mystic Marriage…
may be celebrated and lived…

When one desires the Beloved, there is a fire, a passion. Nothing else in the world will satiate the longing for the Mystic Marriage. No amount of training outwardly will bring the union. Going outward works only if we use it as the gathering of information and inspiration to go within. We must find that place within us that is outside human concepts.

The wedding…it is…
in the garden…
The garden…it is here…
Friends…it is here…
and it is…everywhere…

The Offspring of Fear

When we enter into the sense of separation from our Source, our Self, we automatically begin to experience some degree of fear. For we have lost our connection to our answers, our solutions, our inspirations, our insights, our intuitions, our direct knowings. We have lost our finest impulses. We are lost...and in fear to some degree. With fear is borne a need to control our environment, the seeming outside world. From the perceived need to control is borne the human belief in using and/or manipulating others. That is the spell, the lie, the hypnotism under which much of humanity suffers, suffocates and becomes catatonic, aging and stiffened in depression.

And it is in that moment of sense of separation from our authentic Source of Being that unholy sight is borne. It is in that moment that unholy relationships are borne. It is in that moment that fear takes charge. And love does flee...

The offspring of fear are endless, with one fear companioning and compounding the next. The complexities are great. The endless ensuing pathologies are great. Rising and falling civilizations have been built on those fears. And in fear's wake, greed is borne, causing endless battles and useless, needless wars in home and world community, which feeds and nourishes our bloody recorded history of "taking from others" out of fear.
And culture...it is thwarted and perversed.

Together...we can end this bloody chapter of humanity's unfolding.

Together...we can see that this movement from unholy sight to holy sight shifts the focus from taking from others and controlling others out of fear, to giving to others from the love borne of consciousness of oneness. This giving is accomplished through giving acknowledgment of who the person really is. This giving is accomplished through seeing clearly and purely the Real Self of the other person. It is accomplished by seeing soul to soul. It takes no money to do this, nor even education. It takes willingness to see the soul of another.

And it is done.
The gift is given.

New relationships are borne. They are borne in the home, in local and expanded communities and governing bodies. These new and holy relationships have broken the barriers of race, religion, status and all exclusivity. These new relationships are inclusive of the family of humanity. These new relationships have the climate and tone needed for true culture (cult of UR/gathering of light) at any level to experience the ecstasy of the Oneness that we are.

And it is done.
The gift is given.

Longevity

Beholding Presence as our very Being…is Holy Sight. Presence as our very Being is a true bringer of longevity. For Presence is ageless and timeless. Presence is Light… Presence IS…

Dates, calendars, time are creations of the human mind. They are as figments of the imagination. We do endless things to time to control and manipulate it with our minds. Outside of that mind…Presence is…

Such joy and peace may be ours as we are lifted into these exalted states, outside of time. These states are not meant to be temporary highs, with a lapsing back into the miseries of the human condition. These states are the true life that we may aspire to and attain through earnestness. In these higher states, through meditation, we realize we are light. Each of our cells is light. Our cells are immortal. Our cells do our bidding.

Let us awaken to our true state and identify with it and leave those conditions that so limit the Limitless.

Let us mirror and reflect this limitless Infinite.
Let us be free.
Let us see with Holy Sight…and be free…

As humans, we hope medicine and machines of all kinds will bring longevity. Or even mental power. How can longevity be brought or even bought? It is. It already is.

That state of consciousness awaits our seeing.
It awaits…

Holy Sight...on the road...

It is easy for any of us to drive down a road or a freeway and become irritated, annoyed or even angry at other drivers. And we all know about road rage in our society. Given the wisdom shared by the ancients, as well as the wisdom shared by quantum physicists that we live in a subjective universe, it is becoming more clear that our 'road experience' is 'unfolding consciousness.'

How is it that we can affect a change in this part of our lives that often includes long stretches of driving time?
How is it we can cease attracting negative road experiences?
How is it that we can use 'road time' for illumination and enlightenment?
How is it that freeways can become our ashrams of ceaseless practice?
And how is it that Holy Sight reveals a spiritual universe out upon the roads of the nations?

These questions can all be answered together. It is through a shift in consciousness that our road experience may shift. As within, so without. It is through the awareness created by Holy Sight that the road world may change. This involves the simple law/universal principle of seeing beyond the appearance world. And while the law is simple, practice may not always be, for we are entrenched in our human belief that 'the world is out there.' The outer world actually begins in our consciousness. We can either have human consciousness of miscreation unfolding in our lives or have a higher Consciousness.

There is no 'other' out there on the road. There is only I, the impersonal I, that exists as the One as the Many, the One as individualized form and being. If we so choose, we may practice that Oneness Consciousness with Holy Sight, breaking our malpractice, our spell, by seeing outer personalities in their true spiritual identity. We may actually see past the appearance world of bad driving and see the true spiritual identity of the other driver/drivers. In that, we open up an unprecedented harmony on the road.

Let me give an example. I was driving in rush hour traffic in LA in 6 lanes of fast moving traffic trying to leave work at the end of the day. The driver behind me was merely inches behind me projecting the angry thought of 'go faster' toward me. I was hemmed in by traffic in front and on both sides. I could not change my speed even if I wanted to. My first human inclination was to react and get angry back or even to shake my fist out my moon roof. My emotions and my actions were about to follow my beliefs and thoughts about the situation. I have discovered that I must catch myself quickly. If the human discordant emotion takes hold, it often plays out in a big or small drama. If instead, very quickly one may begin to come into the awareness of 'Presence IS,' there is a shift, sometimes subtle and sometimes grand. Next comes the awareness of 'Presence IS everywhere present' and then extend it to the situation. Presence is manifest as this driver. This is absolutely not used as a mental affirmation. This is used as an awareness that has a felt sense. One may actually feel the driver's Presence and one's own Presence as the One Presence that it is. Harmony happens. Resonance happens. Peace happens. Not from me, but from the 'It that already is."

In that Holy Sight, I stepped out of the battle, invited by the other driver. I stepped out of any opposition, knowing that Presence knows no opposition. Presence knows only of the most precious dance of Beauty. In this Presence, we enact that dance of Oneness at a primordial level, allowing it to surface through this vessel that we are, through this temple template of Infinity that we are.

In the practice of Holy Sight that day on the Los Angeles freeway, the other driver was what seemed to be magically and mystically about five car lengths away from me, as soon as I began to be aware of his inner Presence. There is only one Presence.

We do not need to be hard on ourselves if we do not do this well all the time.
But we can begin.
We can begin.

We can begin to practice Holy Sight. As we practice, we shall get better and better at catching ourselves from reacting to the 'outer seeming.'

In holding the beauty of Holy Sight, we shall behold this internal alchemy appear outwardly as 'our outer world.' We shall witness the quantum physics directly in our own lives. We shall be the beholders of that which reorganizes and restructures our appearance world.

Do we ask often enough about this seeming appearance world? Do we ask the right questions about the physical universe that we live in? Do we take inner time to realize we live as an illumined holographic mandala of Oneness.
Do we realize?
Do we want to realize?
It takes effort and earnestness to realize.
It takes practice to realize.
And Joy is the gift. Exhaltation is the gift.
A new life realized…is the gift.

We all have our difficult moments. Our really human moments. But so what.
We can begin this day. We can begin this day to Realize Oneness on the roads of this nation and of this world.

These roads of the world are as threads of a grander tapestry, all connecting one place to another. These roads of transportation allow global communication. They transport ideas, people, goods and services.
They are passageways of love.
Let us see them so.

Arriving on the road allows the possibility of a highly evolved experience of collective love.
Let us be a part of this shift.

One may actually begin before one leaves the house. Make contact with the Presence, which knows no time or space limitations, and realize it as the activity in all drivers as you prepare to leave on your journey. This mystical contact with Presence allows the Great Mystery to unfold in ways unimagined by the human mind.

Many years ago, I had a comprehensive vision of how collisions happen in consciousness. I saw, as well, a vision of a time when collisions would cease to be. For it is impossible for 'love' to collide and injure. Impossible. Love is an Inviolate Law. Love is Balance and Harmony.
It knows no opposition.
It knows no battle.

And because there is only Consciousness unfolding, let us know that our individual lives and practices and beliefs and concepts matter. They matter not only for our own lives, but for the One Life. Lives lived from Consciousness break the spell, the lie…borne of human false concepts of our selves and one another.

An illumined sword lies within our hearts.
It can pierce the spell cast over much of humanity's seasons.
It can pierce the lies…as if they never were.
Let us use our glowing sword…
Let us behold the beauty of this practice…

Holy Sight Creates Holy Relationships

Holy Sight creates holy relationships and because the Undivided Unmanifest One, manifests as the Divided, it is relevant that we have only holy relationships with everyone and everything.

Should we not understand clearly the principle that the Undivided and Unmanifest One/God manifests as the seeming myriad many that we know as Life, then we may find ourselves living a life of a seeming sense of separation that is full of human pain and fear. We must want to know and experience Creator as Creation. Creator is manifest as all of Creation and that is the exalted joy of being here on this planet.

Friends, we are the experiencer of this One come as the Many. It is the gift. As we extend Holy Sight to the Many, we shall quickly discover that that Holy Sight creates holy relationships. This Holy Sight creates sacred relatings no matter where we are, who we are with or what we are doing. The world cannot resist Holy Sight for Holy Sight is the acknowledgment of the truth of a person, place or thing.

Every relationship of any kind has the potential of being transformed with Holy Sight. There is no area of our lives at home, office, studio, nature, social that it is not deeply purposeful. We may be creative in our practice. It does not matter where or with whom we find ourselves with now.

Should a person not be receptive to Holy Sight, either they or you will not desire to be in one another's presence. Circumstances and situations and/or awareness will arise to have you very naturally part ways. Everyone is entitled to free will and their belief in false concepts about themselves. Allow. Holy Sight does not control nor manipulate. It is an honoring of the other person's Authentic Self.

In some cases, it may take time, for the person to respond to Holy Sight, so deeply embedded are the lies/spells of miscreation. Be patient as you hold space for another's awareness of their illumined self to begin to emerge.

Even with our children, it may take time. It matters not the time. For what we practice now…is a living in the eternal…in the timeless realm…of what is…what already is.
We cannot even indulge in the thought that we are healing the person. We are merely healing our own vision of the person, to seeing what IS, what already IS.

This practice of Holy Sight is a practice of the awareness of the One Presence animating all of the manifest world. After we can feel this Presence in ourself, we extend this awareness into the seeming external world. In that, we have begun our practice of creating holy relationship.

One may begin in a way that is easy. Begin in nature. Perhaps begin with a stone or a butterfly or a wildflower or even with the wind or the stars in the sky. As you extend Holy Sight, you become aware of the Soul Presence in all things. Say you are beholding a mountain stream. Bring acute sensitivity and awareness to beholding the soul of the stream. You may do this with all the kingdoms and the elements. It is a powerful moment when you face a stone soul to soul. I have done this and heard the stones sing at the river's edge. Being aware of Presence as the stones has inspired much of my mystical art. In meditation, they have appeared in the Archetypal Realms revealing shapeshifting faculties. The experiences awaiting us are endless…

At one point, I consciously created a loving relationship with a fly, soul to soul. It sat beside me as I painted, prepared food and as I lived my life. It shared its delight with our interspecies communication. One person and one insect in the relationship of Oneness. My heart would open at its appearance each day in my world.

I have had endless animal visitations. One morning at dawn I was overshawdowed by the presence of Spotted Owl. It gave me very practical instructions and messages about its survival in the forests of the west coast of America. I carried out all of the instruction. Through Holy Sight, we increase our communication and may become the voice of any and many animals that so need that assistance.

We can even have holy relationship with weather. Weather mirrors consciousness. For many years of working with clients in the area of Consciousness, we have observed the remarkable reflection of weather and nature. I have witnessed the endless synchronicity of weather/nature interacting at profound moments of awakening in sessions and workshops. It may come in the form of birds, clouds, rainbows, deer, wind. It may come in any form. In the moment that it comes, it is unquestionably clear that it arises to speak directly to the moment of the timeless experience, seeming to happen in time. It is a precious moment…usually never to be repeated again.

Some of the most profound Holy Sight experiences are with those who we may have regarded as enemies or opponents on earth's stage. I have seen extremely dramatic changes in my life and in the lives of clients with such ones. One of the most dramatic in my own personal life was with my father. I began to practice Holy Sight on my father when I was in my 30's. I had many torrid experiences with my father, who was a raging and violent alcoholic who abused woman in general at every opportunity in many forms. As a child, I even prayed to God very often to have my father die in a plane crash so he would not return home and hurt my mother again. When I finally learned well the principle involved with Holy Sight, I began to deeply practice. Each time I became aware of my father, I would practice. Again and again I would practice. It was not easy.
It was difficult. It was not easy to see such a cruel person as 'Light manifest'. It was painfully difficult at times.

And then changes began to happen. My father who lived thousands of miles away called me for the first time in my adult life. Then he told me he loved me for the first time in my life. Then he began to come and visit me and my daughters for the first time in my life. Then he began to give me gifts for the first time in my life. Then he began to inquire constantly if there was anything we needed. My father changed. My father changed because I changed how I saw him. My father had a place inside of him that was still open. He responded. I never did ask him why he had been so violent and cruel.

I just went with the manifestation that matched my higher vision of my father. Such is the law of the universe.

Another story happened in relation to my mother. My mother was an alcoholic until about the age 70. I had been deeply practicing Holy Sight with my mother. She began to call me almost each time that I was practicing. At first I told her I had been thinking about her when she called. Later I told her that I had been doing this practice and she wanted to know what it was. After the sharing, her sensitivity and awareness grew. She would call and say, 'You can do that thing on me anytime. I like it and I can feel when you are doing it.' After more time passed, she called me and asked me to instruct her how to do Holy Sight for herself. The moment that my mother died, she came to me as a blazing ball of light into the space around my head. I had to communicate to her how to go into the Light and merge with it as her very own self.

Our worlds may change.

The Global Picture

Because of the realization that "the world is within," that it is our very consciousness, there is no possibility of viewing the global condition, of human fear, pain and misery and the impurity in the air, water, earth and food, the same. In this case, the mental pollution of humanity has created the problems of pollution in the kingdoms and the elements.

It may sound like a grand over simplification. It is not. Should we even ask a child dwelling in the awe and wonder of the beauty of this planet how we might solve the problem of the impure food, we would inevitably hear something like, "do not poison the earth with chemicals at all." As a humanity, if we should really reach into our soul for solutions, we shall find them. We shall then need to enact them.

As we hold space "of the world within"…as whole and perfect…the outpicturing of that in our lives shall begin. Holding inner sacred space for this global wholeness allows an internal alchemy to transpire. In this, the world is made new.

As it is, we have bought the concept of a world plagued with wars, sins, disease and death. We are subject to our own beliefs. We may clear those concepts that are the equivalent of mental pollution and allow Holy Sight to reveal the Real. In that illumination does a new world, a new culture, a new global picture emerge.

It is not always easy to do this. We are bombarded by the media with pictures of unholy sight. In our humanness, we react and now are part of the problem as we fight and battle against the picture in front of us as physical reality.

We can be inspired by great ones, who instead of reacting went within and received inspiration and inner guidance in the form of direct knowing. Gandhi used this means of studying sacred scriptures and turning within to pray for guidance. Each day he lived the vision. He was acting from inspiration, not reacting from judgment. There is a vast distinction between action and reaction. India was set free. Gandhi did not lead people to freedom from slavery; he led people into a collective freedom in Spirit. His was a spiritual movement, though outwardly it looked to be political. This man was divinely inspired. He was not mentally motivated with some political ideology that would control people. He understood true freedom.

We can, each of us, be inspired from within and given vision and come forth to enact that vision. We are blessed to have knowledge of going within. We are blessed to know that we need not live out our lives as reactionaries and thus be in battle with externals. Let us one by one come forth and live the vision as we receive it.

Together...let us realize that in the Oneness, there is but One Vision and that it plays out in harmonious unity and diversity simultaneously. It is the ever present play of the One as the Many in manifestation. And we are the players.

Let us play.
Let us know that each person matters.
We are Consciousness.
We are Consciousness unfolding.

Human consciousness of miscreation shall give way to Vision for it is God Consciousness unfolding. And it is the only power.

Let us not be imprisoned with false beliefs and concepts.
Let us not wage war with the external world.
Let us deeply contact the Peace that lives within our hearts and let it flow. It shall dissolve the strife, but we must do it and we do it by making contact within, in the silence.

Globally we are at the brink of a collective shift. That is because enough conscious awareness has turned within. Let us feel the inspiration of this inner Vision. It carries within it the strength to bring it forth. That strength is not ours. It is a quality, an attribute from this current of life.

We can embrace Holy Sight of the world and watch, behold and witness the changes or we can continue to view the external world as the reality and enter into unholy sight and become the victims of our very own viewing and perception.

With Holy Sight for the earth, we can come out from under the spell of humanity's miscreations.

Holy Sight and other Realms

As a human species, lost often in the human mind, we have created a deeply limited world, civilization after civilization. Here and there each of us have small or large glimpses outside of these mental prisons. In those moments of such a glimpse, often inspiration followed by great passion does arise in our souls. And our lives are lifted. For some it happens quickly. For others more slowly.

In those glimpses, Holy Sight arises naturally. It is just there. It exists as natural vision. It is both vision of wholeness and holiness. It is revealed as something that does not even need to be practiced. Outside the concepts of the human mind, Holy Sight is experienced as awareness. We have all heard of near death experiences in cars, surgeries, diseases and other forms of tragedies, where another world is experienced. Each person "comes back," so to speak, with a personal story of their awareness that there is nothing but love. That awareness is Holy Sight.

I was in such a collision in 1971, while I was driving on a back road to work on a snowy day. The driver coming toward me went out of control in the snow and hit my car head on. Just before the moment of impact, I heard myself say, "God, I am yours." At the moment of impact I was in Holy Sight. I saw my past, present and future through the eyes of the soul. I was in a purest joy. I saw that I was not manifesting my truth. I saw that I had a new life. I quit my position as an English Instructor at a college. I began to paint; I began to travel nationally and internationally. I began to have Holy Sight by seeing the soul of all of those I met as I traveled in Africa, Greece, Crete, Turkey, Iran, Afghanistan, Pakistan, India and Kashmir. A new life emerged.

We do not need to wait for tragedy, collisions, diseases and accidents to have the glimpse into the world of "there is nothing but love." We can discover that there is nothing but the One, doing the dance of love. Love's dance is all there is.

I would like to share one of my many experiences of Holy Sight and other realms. For years, I lived in a home high on a hill overlooking a valley and a mountain. By that time, through meditation and earnest longing, I had opened to inner sight and hearing. I would at times hear the music of the spheres, with chords and tones beyond imagining of the mind. I was lifted into epiphanies of soul joy. On the property of my home, there also lived a male and female owl. They would call to each other in the night. Precious calls and responses floated through the air. I would inwardly see them and their sounds illumined. I would see their songs ripple as light through the darkened predawns. I would allow my light of self to merge with their illumined songs. I merged and became one with the sweetest songs of love hanging in the air. The joy was often almost greater than my human self could contain. Later I began to hear the inner music of the spheres with inner hearing. I would experience that as illumined and again allow my light to merge with its light, increasing my joy. Later, I learned to simultaneously merge with the owls' calls and the inner music. So the inner music of the spheres and the outer music of nature's owls was now blended. The sound was an exquisite and rapturous song of the Infinite in an ever changing form.

Friends, these experiences await us.

I have many times had the experience of hearing the wind and the wind through the trees as illumined motion, merging with the inner music of the spheres. The upliftment of Spirit cannot be expressed in words. It is the Unspeakable. Even now, my voicing is only to give rise to inspiration of the unlimited ways that humanity may experience.

Following are a few words about sexuality and Holy Sight. Sex is many things to many people, cultures and nations. Holy Sight as a practice in sexuality lifts it into other realms and infinite possibilities. Practicing Holy Sight for self and the other allows an illumined sharing. The mystical opens and stands naked and revealed. Adding words here, adds nothing. Humanity has much to experience and learn from the One, manifest as man and woman, merging as One. A new day arises for humanity. Sex will no longer be experienced as lower chakra; it will be experienced as the illumined sharing of cosmic existence between partners in higher purpose. It is a portal into cosmic consciousness…when Holy Sight is known and deeply practiced.

Let us take these few examples and compound them in our own lives by the simple practice of Holy Sight. Let us each allow the limitless possibilities of Oneness to arise in our own lives. Let us then offer these at the feet of humanity, as a foundation for the building of a real culture borne of the knowledge of love, the law of balance.

I was profoundly affected by the life of my daughter's cat, Porsche, who I cared for when my daughter went through college and other of life's experiences. Porsche became sick over many months and died quite young. I was so grieved by her death that it took me for weeks into deep meditations. My Holy Sight for this cat opened many doors I never imagined. I was transported into the soul realm of animals where I experienced them as already Christed soul. It was magic. It was pure. They revealed themselves as the pure souls that they are. They gave me messages and poems. I could scarcely contain the levels of joy of the experience. Sometimes I would return to my daily consciousness and wail about the inability to hold the exalted awareness of who they really are.

One day in meditation, via Holy Sight, Porsche came to me, then turned and walked my consciousness into the deepest forest where she began shapeshifting into lion, tiger, panther and more. She revealed to me the tribe of cat. She revealed to me their desire to be in nature. She revealed to me their desire to touch the pads of their paws on the earth. She revealed their wildness. I was awed by her ability to unveil reality and communicate with no words. The direct telepathy was a perfect transmission. I was left with no doubt and with no questions.

Porsche's visits and those visits of other animals were initiations into greater recognition of the Oneness. Sometime after that, I began to awaken in the dawns around 4 a.m. and I would write the voices of the animals as poems that would arise. These poems are now a recording called, *Return to Oneness.*

I would add here that many people who are addicted to drugs are trying through chemical and other means to recreate these vast experiences of the Oneness, which are a dim memory in the mind of the collective that we are.

It is time that we remember.
We can remember directly…
and lift the fog of unknowing.
We can lift the seeming thought of separation.
And as humanity begins to remember naturally through Holy Sight, the desire for drugs will cease to be, as if it never were.

Humanity is pointed and poised in this direction.
Humanity must learn that it does not have to create collective wars and crisis to open to the feelings of love, of the Oneness that we are as one spiritual family.

Let us begin this day…
Together…let us begin…

Beauty of Being

Humanly we regard beauty as physical.

Spiritually we regard beauty as inner, a soul quality.

We make the mistake of often identifying with our physical body, judging it and end up abhorring it. There are many reasons for 'the why' that we do this. One is that we may compare ourselves with others; another is that our unknowing separation from 'perfection itself' may have created the manifestation of imperfect thoughts.

A powerful way to break this false identity is to sit down, get comfortable, breathe slowly and enter the Silence. When you feel you have made contact with this inner Stillness that may take a minute or an hour, keep your eyes closed a bit longer.

Do the following prayer. Do it with words or wordlessly. (Do not make the mistake of using this prayer like an affirmation that is usually a repetitive mental exercise.) To have a lasting effect, you must experience and feel the statement. It is, 'I breathe beauty of being into expression.' Feel it. As you continue to feel it, watch all of your concepts and judgments of yourself come flying into your mind, demanding to be heard and acted upon. Witness those thoughts, but do not entertain or indulge them. Stay at one with the truth of beauty of being. It is a state of consciousness. It is an experience. You can come to feel it in every cell. It is the 'as within, so without.'

We may even have thoughts and remembrances of where we received those negative and imperfect thoughts about ourselves. A parent, a child in schoolyard, a sibling. The list can be endless of those who unmercifully judged us according to outer appearance. The human tragedy is that we claimed their thought as our own and built part of our life around it. Now is the time for a disclaimer. Now is the time to be in holy communion, in the grandest church of all, yourself. Now is the time to realize the body as your temple.

Now is the time to embrace your beauty of being, that all thoughts to the contrary, may dissolve as the nothingness that they are. These thoughts have been your masters and they have imprisoned your precious splendor. These thoughts have kept you in the spell of matter. They are the pathologies of a mind in separation. They are a mind that does not yet know Holy Sight.

Merge now with the following as a state of conscious awareness.
'I breathe beauty of being into expression.'
Feel that.
It is subtle.
Feel it and thus know it.
Behold that as so.
Now slowly, when ready, open your eyes. Look around. As you begin to notice your environment, stay simultaneously aware of Beauty of Being as your very own self. Our outer environment might become our greatest teacher of this remembrance. Each temptation to sway from experiencing deep Beauty of Being is the world initiating you into mastery. Be grateful for the teachers. The ones closest to us are the most difficult, but they make us wax strong in the attainment of this state of consciousness.

'I breathe beauty of being into expression.' We want that as our reality. It is reality. We want it for our very self. There is only one self, so when we begin to extend that awareness of 'beauty of being in expression everywhere.' we initiate a powerful alchemy. Because, we too, have judged other forms; we have imprisoned ourselves in the spell of good and bad. We have become the ones who unknowingly malpractice others. We hide, cover and disguise these thoughts with thoughts such as 'I perceive.' When we finally comprehend that those thoughts are not true and that we receive the return of those thoughts as a boomerang, we shall long to stop those thoughts and we shall enter Holy Sight. We will extend vision of beauty of being to ourselves and selves everywhere, regardless of how ignorant or unillumined they may seem.

This is the alchemy of 'do unto others what you would have them do unto you.' This is not a biblical or religious platitude. It is scientific. It is universal law. When followed, it will transform our lives and touch all those about us.

'I breathe beauty of being into expression.' We constantly try to balance our chemistry, our hormones, our bodies, minds and emotions by diet, herbs and medicine. This may all be helpful, but let us not forget that our thoughts create imbalances that wreak havoc on our mental, emotional and physical bodies. And sometimes to add something externally is only a temporary fix, until we recognize the internal alchemy of our thoughts.

Let us together… turn to the inner alchemist…
Let us together… go to this only source of balance…
Let us find sanctuary in this sweetness…
Let us play this harp of forever and
bask in the light of beauty of being…

Holy Sight and Legal Issues

When Holy Sight is truly understood and practiced widespread, legal issues will begin to dwindle and finally they shall cease to be. In 1999, I became deeply aware of how Holy Sight might affect legal issues and lawsuits no matter the scale of it. Ones who heard about my work with Holy Sight began to share about their legal trouble and/or lawsuit in which they were enmeshed. As I listened to each person who came to me, I realized that the Holy Sight, as a spiritual principle, was still the perfect way to approach the seeming problem confronting the person. I could see that it did not matter that there was the accused, the accuser, attorneys, witnesses, jury and judge.

Essentially what we witness humanly is very simple. It is a battle of right and wrong. It is a battle. And we are battling. We are at war. Embroiled in the situation, we may easily fill with extreme fear and become angry, anxious, resentful, powerless, victimized.
We need not travel that road of the eons old battle of duality.

What I share with each person is very simple. It is only the complexities of the battle of good and bad, of duality, that seem without solution. With each person, I share some main ideas that must be understood and practiced. They are aspects of practicing Holy Sight.

1. Be willing to leave the battle in relationship to the existing seeming problem.
2. Be willing to live beyond fear by rising in consciousness to a realm where fear dwells not.
3. Be willing to see through and beyond the seeming and appearing human traits of a person, knowing that beyond those, is the pure and true essence of their Being. Be willing to contact that.
4. Be willing to see that those accusing persons are outpicturing their human concepts and opinions about the world and their life.

5. Be willing to shift and see the inner truth of Being of all involved in the case. Be willing to know Presence in those others.

6. Be aware that your shift from human consciousness to Consciousness creates an alchemy, in which seeming miracles and magic may occur.
   Allow this alchemy.
   What really happens is that grace occurs.
   Beauty of Being happens.

7. Be willing to leave the idea of winning and losing.

One must understand that to 'fight the case' means to enter in at the level of those who have taken the role of opposition. Then one is very simply…a part of the battle and the problem. When one understands that to leave the battle means to set in motion the alchemy of grace, then Grandness happens.
Joy occurs.
Answers and solutions appear.
The battle…it does end…

For regardless of the nature of the battle, there is a possibility of practicing the Holy Sight and coming into deep inner Oneness with all the ones that are involved in the case. With the practice and experience of the inner Oneness, outer changes do occur.

Many of the changes that I have seen in such cases have been startling and unexpected. This is because, in the Oneness, there is no opposition. There is no battle.

One person in a lawsuit in a courtroom, was face to face with the one who had falsely accused. This accused person had been practicing Holy Sight. In that supreme sight, the accuser could no longer hold the position of the lie and broke into tears, hugging the accused and apologizing. The lawsuit ended quickly, leaving the accused with not even an attorney to pay.

In another huge lawsuit, someone was falsely accused in a business disagreement. The accused practiced Holy Sight, even though the Labor Union was the seeming adversary. Once the accused left the battle and left the realm of fear, the lawsuit ended quite easily and without large damages.

Another person in a property battle actually had a friendship with the 'seeming opposition' emerge. This is not a miracle; it is life lived in love. Holy Sight does extend love into the world and to the so called enemy of the lawsuit.

In one case, there was a battle over family land. Just one person in this drama of siblings was practicing Holy Sight. That one person shifted the energy. Family members no longer cared about the outcome of the case. They were now finding new ways to relate. The thought around the case was no longer about winning. Just one person affected all the others. Love emerged.

There is no reason to go into the details of these cases, for the only thing that matters is the awareness of the changes that come from practicing Holy Sight. The important ingredient is in the practice of seeing the illumined self of others. In that, change…it comes.

The world of judges, courtrooms and lawsuits may shift into understanding, borne of the consciousness of Oneness, which is outside of fear and separation from source.

A heaven world awaits us in this shift.
It is ours.
It awaits our seeing.
It awaits our willingness.
It awaits.

We can begin to see that the practice of Holy Sight has to begin with someone. Otherwise the battle rages through our history and through the long eons creating scars between families and nations.

Someone must first understand Holy Sight.
Someone must practice the principle.
Someone must leave judgment and revenge and fear behind.
Someone must leave the past behind and never look back.
Someone must choose Holy Sight…which allows forgiveness.

And the world…it changes.

We have forgotten that we live in a thought wave universe. We have forgotten that our thoughts outpicture as our very lives. We have forgotten how creation happens.

Together…let us remember.
Let us remember that we are One.
Let us remember Creator as Creation.

Let us understand others and have compassion.
Let us know that others are outpicturing the beliefs taught and given to them.
When we penetrate that conceptual universe and see others as they truly are, that which we know as the physical universe may change, shift and uplift.

Justice prevails…
for justice is…
Justice is balance lived…

We need not become politicians, historians or even scholars to affect change.
We may affect change…simply…very simply…by practicing this universal principle of Holy Sight… which extends love into the world.

Practice: Holy Sight for Others

As I awakened more deeply into Holy Sight in the 1970's, I began to see that every moment of every day was an opportunity to practice Holy Sight. I began to see that every moment was a sacred moment and every moment was an opportunity to penetrate the human conceptual universe and come into Presence.

I was filled with strong impulses to spend time practicing in some very specific ways. I would take long walks in my community and practice Holy Sight. I would drive to town, park and begin to walk. I practiced Holy Sight with everyone and anyone. I came to see many moments of the sweetest beauty. People walking down the street in deep sadness or depression would look up as they passed by. Our eyes would meet. We would for an instant commune soul to soul. I could feel them shift. I could feel their upliftment.

All this…done in a glance…
All this…so simple…
All this…available to all…

Practicing Holy Sight is not about control or manipulation on any level of consciousness. It is about grace. It is about allowing life to unfold in holy and unprecedented ways.

With years of practice while walking, driving, being at home and on, another experience began to unfold in my life. I would be walking in town and feeling the Presence that animates me. As I practiced Holy Sight, I was aware of Presence animating all others. As I deepened my ability to extend the awareness of the Presence to those around me, I would feel myself to be part of an 'illumined holographic mandala,' always moving, changing and unique, while also being harmonious and in communion. In these moments I feel both individual and personal, while paradoxically fully impersonal. We are the same Essence, Substance of everyone and everything. This holographic mandala experience which I both behold and simultaneously am a part of...is like a living kaleidoscope. That is the All come forth as the Many.

We may practice Holy Sight in all parts of our lives. We may be creative and see that each experience has its gifts. No matter how difficult the situation, we have the possibility to rise above the realm of problems and allow Holy Sight to shapeshift the situation. And grace descends.

We may practice this with friends, family, colleagues, strangers. We may even practice with seeming enemies. It is best when we use it each time life gives us a problem, an obstacle. We can actually learn to be in love with the problem. It is for growth.
It is ultimately for our joy.

We can turn our lives around.
We can live in exultation.
We can love our life.

This does not mean that everyone will respond to our Holy Sight and come closer to us. Those who are not open to this way of being seen may actually shun us, or leave our presence or even disappear from our lives. This may be for a short time or a long time. It does not matter.

Our only responsibility is to practice the principle and behold its activity in and as our very lives. In such clarity do we begin to see that unholy sight brings bondage. In the wake of bondage is bred pain, suffering, limitation and the growth of endless fear.

Let us no more indulge in unholy sight.
Let us no longer indulge in an act that can seep into our lineages and keep family and international wars in continuance for centuries or even eons.

With Holy Sight the battles of the ages do end...
With Holy Sight does come a precious knowledge of union...
With Holy Sight our arms do open...

Holy Sight and Wholeness

We need to attain Holy Sight for ourselves and others in order that we can have health and wholeness in our own lives. Each subtle nuance of a thought of self and other selves, that are the same self, either enhances and enriches us and them or destroys us.

We affect every fiber of our Being through Holy Sight or unholy sight. And the choice is ours, no matter how difficult the present moment, situation or condition is. Unholy sight sets in motion the creation of toxins into our system and bloodstream. Holy Sight does illumine each cell that is a vessel of the Infinite.

Let us detox with the beauty of Holy Sight.
Beauty does unveil itself to us everywhere.
in a blade of grass…
in the blowing winds…
in the fading flower…
    that returns but a moment…
    only to bloom again…
everywhere…beauty dances…
beauty dances naked to those who can see…

This passage can only reveal its truth with practice. Practice of Holy Sight shall cleanse and purify our mind and thus our manifested world of time and space.

And Beauty…SHE…shall appear.

Holy Sight and Romance

To begin this passage, we must have a deep understanding of what true romance is. I am not speaking of the glamorized Hollywood false sense of romance that often reflects the great imbalance of the ages. That has helped to turn people from the knowing of true romance, that is the equilibrium of Archetypal and Original HE and SHE. History is full of the suffering borne of man and woman coming together for all of the wrong reasons. Some of these reasons are status, financial gain, social gain, ancestral rules, religions dogma, caste systems, loneliness, lust and ruling classes that include governments. The true story in the movie, *Dangerous Beauty*, reveals the impact of church and state in erecting barriers historically to guard the coming together of true love. In this movie, that happened in Venice, Italy, we see state and church have been a part of the division of woman into four distinct areas. A woman could be a subservient maid, a nun, a chaste and uneducated and unadorned mother, or a highly educated and adorned courtesan, schooled perfectly in the art of whoring. Love simply could not fulfill the true pairing intended in this electrically sexed universe. Union of true love has been blocked in so many ways. The Law of Balance is inviolate, yet it has been violated in so many forms.

I will speak now of the union of man and woman who are truly matched and brought together by the cosmic law of balance. They are magnetized by a higher force and have a higher purpose. They see one another. They behold one another. They honor one another. Their union uplifts them into a realm of unprecedented sharing and opens them to the receiving of the new cosmology. It opens them to the receiving of ideals and the landing of those ideals to create new culture, not the repeated rising and falling of imbalanced and savage civilizations borne of imbalanced mating. The world must awaken to partners in purpose. These partners have a holy calling.

The 'Partners in Purpose' are the solution to the ending of the rising and falling of imbalanced civilizations. They are the foundation of the emerging new world. From these sacred partners, comes an illumined culture. The word culture comes from the ancient words, cult and UR, meaning gathering of light.

The 'Partners in Purpose' have inherent in their relating Holy Sight for one another. They have inherent in their relating a precious beholding. They are balanced and equal.
These relatings are borne of a higher impulse. Let us know that these sacred partners are the birthers of the new world. They are not just one man and one woman equals two; they are one plus one equals Infinity.

Together...do they land the new world...
Together...do they land the garden...
Together...do they live those fairy tales that were rarely told, for they were rarely lived...
Together...do they constitute the balance that the world has rarely seen...
Together...do they herald and enact world balance...

How many man/woman unions do you know that are ecstatic, that are noble and exemplary? How many man/woman unions do you know that could model for the building of a culture borne of balance. The ones who have done this made contact with the Holy Presence, the pure essence of light within, knowing that that Oneness must then outpicture itself as one's outer world. The world is within.

This coming together of balanced man and woman is the principle of yin and yang in equal measure. It is a law that operates in all of nature and all processes of nature. It can be seen everywhere as we step into the mystical nature that awaits our seeing.

Holy Sight and Romance is the starting point of an emerging new world. It is the foundation for World Balance. Man and woman in balance extend this balance into the home, community, village, city, county, nation and civilization that they might pass through the need for falling, decaying, degrading and self destructing for lack of balance.

Once one receives even a glimpse of this inviolate law of balance needed to be lived in the man/woman world, one begins to see the obvious. This principle becomes obvious. It becomes astonishing to see how we have allowed such imbalance, when all that is happening in the world is the undivided, invisible and unmanifest One unveiling and manifesting as the divided and visible Two, the HE and She of all Creation, the Yin and Yang of all of nature and the processes of nature. These polarities are not in opposition. They are very simply the manifest dance of the One.

Today...let us enter this dance...
Today...let us have a glimpse...
Today...let us feel the exaltation of this union...
Today...let us lift our sight...
   ...let us attain holy sight and romance...
   ...let us be the pillars of an unprecedented world...

We can be a part of a world of imbalance and a failing life and civilization or we can work with the principle of balance and be part of an emerging world of joy.

Beginning in the 1980's in meditation, I have been uplifted with inner vision to see the truth of this principle of balance. I repeatedly was called into realms of Archetypal and Original He and She.

On one occasion, meditating at the base of Mt Whitney, I was invited into the cosmic mouth and allowed to behold a Holy Procession of sacred partners down through the ages. It is nearly unspeakable. I now voice a few words to illumine the awareness of these ecstatic unions. I did behold the procession of Archetypal HE and SHE in many cultures, races and forms. These forms included the beauty of the Two by Twos. I was given to know that the Twos carry the energy and power of Infinity. I saw that the new world was emerging two by two. I saw these unions exalted as prince and princess, king and queen, priest and priestess, shaman and shamaness, seer and seeress. I saw the Beauty beyond measure of their being and their union. Truly, the mystical marriage made manifest as man and woman, as god/goddess.

I could scarcely contain the immensity of the beauty and power of these twos. In the ecstasy of knowing was paradoxically the awareness of the pain of humanity borne of imbalance.

Since age four, I have had a glimmer of awareness about the existence of the sacred partners. As a child, I had no intellectual understanding. I did not have conscious knowledge of the eternal yin/yang principle. I had only some sort of dim knowing of what seemed to me to be magical relationshiops. The principle began to unveil itself in exalted realms in meditations, leaving me free of doubt.

What I witnessed, is the world of balance wanting manifestation in this world. I saw into the substance of creation where only epiphany dwells. In each, I was given vast teachings which I have brought forth as mystic art, poetry, multi-media sacred enactments, dance, sounds and sessions, retreats and workshops. I saw the Feminine as keeper of Vision. In my recording and multimedia event, *SHE...it is...who Remembers,* I have shared many of the gifts that SHE, the receptive does bring to help bring world balance.

Let us connect...with that inner knowing...that the romance of the eternal may materialize on this spinning orb we know as earth.

In Holy Sight and Romance...is the disappearance forever of all battles and wars and the violating of the law of balance.

Sessions and Workshops

For many years I have shared Soul Remembering sessions and retreats with individuals and groups all around the globe. Contained in those gatherings have been the understanding and practice of Holy Sight. In the last few years, those sessions and retreats expanded into The Holy Sight workshop.

I speak of this now, because as I expanded into working with groups, instead of just individuals, I was able to witness the Infinite at work in a new way. I witnessed the increased activity and power of 'two or more gathered together.'

I began by teaching each workshop participant how to 'hold space,' that is, how to stay in the Holy Presence and how to extend that awareness to others. In extending that awareness, one dissolves the human concept and opinions of the others, penetrates the finite sense of others, and arrives at the inner awareness of who the other really IS. It allows a distinct knowingness of the divinity of the seeming other. It allows one to know that person as the manifestation of the One Soul.

When one person, in the center of the group circle at the workshop, is really being seen by all who are present, an internal alchemy begins. Quantum physics, then, is no stranger. Mystical as practical is no longer as stranger. The person in the center of the circle begins to shift in consciousness and transform. An upliftment happens and all who can feel the current of Presence can feel the shift. The entire group is uplifted in the measure of that knowing. For we are One.
It is not supernatural, paranormal or magic.
It is Principle/Cosmic Law manifest.
It is simple.
It is inviolate.

I would like to share a few of the types of experiences that occur through Holy Sight. This work is experiential. It is about change, growth, love, revelation.

One woman came to me who was a vivacious and strong being in the world. When she arrived to do the Holy Sight work, she described herself as almost totally dysfunctional in the world. The reason for this state was because of her hatred for Osama Ben Ladin, which began to grow and fester in her as she listened to national news reports teaching her to hate this man. She followed the instructions, like a child in school, and learned to hate with great intensity. That hate traveled through her brain, her cells and through her very veins. She was the life of the very hatred that she expressed. And now it lived in her. She was able to painfully experience the return of the thought of revenge. And she learned that any hate that she sends out must travel through her first. With time she attained the understanding of why she needed to do Holy Sight, which was for her to look beyond the human appearance and see the holy being residing inside this man. That was the only way she could get out of the bondage that she herself was now in.

When we began the work of Holy Sight, this woman felt a fiery current of energy return to her in grand amounts. It was like the wave of an ocean. The human thought that she had cast, returned to her as the LOVE that she already IS. She had been in great bondage to her very thoughts of hatred. In returning to love, she was free in Presence. And she saw in that purity of love that she had been part of the international teaching of hatred and battle. She saw that she was now outside of even a need to forgive. In the recognition of truth of being of another, forgiveness has already happened. It is already done.

In another instance, a woman hated a national politician and all that he was doing in creating international war. Holy Sight for this seeming evil person was difficult for this woman. With the help of Holy Sight from the circle of people in the workshop, this woman was not only lifted beyond the human rage, but was given a revelation of this man as a frightened child, who could act no other way than out of fear. She had her heart open toward him; compassion visited and she was gifted with new insight of how to relate to such ones that are imprisoned in the fear dwelling in their own minds.

In one workshop, someone said that they had felt disconnected from their own Soul for a long time. As the group worked with Holy Sight, this person witnessed the leaving of insidious thought forms from her self. A clearing occurred without anyone ever even knowing that that was what was being called for. Holy Sight is Presence in action in our lives.

Holy Sight is love expressed and extended to one another.
Holy Sight is divine alchemy.
Holy Sight has been missing from the world.

No matter what our gifts, talents, economics, we can give the gift of Holy Sight. It is in giving that we are regiven. That is the law.

When we gift Holy Sight to another, we are looking past outer appearance and seeing only the truth of illumined being. We are seeing their authentic self that already IS. In that, we have enacted the true meaning of the word education. Education is an ancient Greek word meaning 'to draw out that which is already within.' Let us all be true educators and be the ones who can see that Love is appearing in myriad forms as the kingdoms and elements of the earth play.

Another workshop participant said she came to the workshop to deal with an issue with a man with whom she had been involved. She gave no details. As she sat in the middle of the group, describing her own personal plight of emotions, she came to the deep realization that she needed to do Holy Sight for all men, for Archetypal Original Man. And she realized that she was doing it for her own sake, not for theirs. She realized that her generalized thoughts of man was outpicturing and appearing in her world. In that changed vision of man, this woman changed.

The seeming subtlety of thought in this thought wave, light wave universe turns out not to be so subtle.

During a New Mexico retreat, I had a deeper initiation into the creative process of creator and humanity. I could for a brief time feel and sense the collective thought forms of humanity's creating. I took some moments and wailed for us all in that knowing. Compassion entered me and I moved beyond the stage of wailing and saw what to humanity seems as the logic and reason of the beliefs and opinions held so tightly. We must individually and then collectively pass through the 'field of excuses to hate' and enter into the realm of love. We must deeply and profoundly desire to give Love a body. That body can be the simple glance of Holy Sight flowing to another. No longer will there be the evil eye.

Let us harken unto this call of Love. It is a gift that can be given anytime, anywhere and with anyone. It can even be given when we are fully alone and solitary. We can extend Holy Sight from our minds and it travels across this thought wave universe of ours, just as do the sounds, pictures and thoughts of television, computers, radios, cell phones, psychics, telepaths and readers.

We are all a part of this One Mind. As we learn to live in Holy Sight, our human mind becomes a transparency for this One Mind. No longer are there distortions and perversions of this Love. And each of us matters in giving Holy Sight one person to another, one nation to another and one race to another.

I Am Everywhere

Let us together…make a passage…a grand odyssey…
to the smallest…to the biggest…to the
closest and the farthest…to the Everywhere…
Let us hear the voice of everything…from everywhere…

The sand whispers from deserts and island shores…
    I Am here…walk upon me…
The leaves softly blow and speak…
    I Am here…come stand in my shade…
and the mountains…they shout…
    I Am above…come unto me
        come unto my summit…
And the rocks…they do sing…
    I Am here…listen…you shall hear…I am Soul…
And everyplace we do turn…we listen…
    each animal…
    and each plant…
Each one speaks…I Am here…
And the fire…the metal…the water…
    all the elements …each has a voice…
I Am here…and I commune with you…
    for we are One…

What is this grand I Am that speaks from so many forms and faces
and places?
What is the voice that is everywhere present?

With Holy Sight…we acknowledge this
    illumined Presence…
    and It may speak…
    It has a voice…
    It is Life…

And finally do we realize...that...
    I Am Everywhere...Present...
        and
    I Am the only Presence Here...

We do realize this presence is everywhere present.
We do realize that we may connect with and merge
with this light of Presence in everything.

Let us extend this knowing to everything,
whether animate or inanimate. It is all the
One Soul, appearing as the Many.
The One as the Many.

I had been practicing Holy Sight for many years. One day I was traveling down I-5 from Mount Shasta to work in Los Angeles. I had entered the sanctity of the Angeles National Forest, just north of Los Angeles, as I had on many work journeys south. The cars were flying by; the noise was great. Yet a Silence that I had never noticed in quite that way began to pervade my awareness. I felt as if I were entering a world devoid of time...and ecstasy...it did arise in me. Joy traveled freely through my veins and great brilliance touched every cell.

Out of this Stillness...I clearly heard the words...

    I Am Everywhere...Present...
        and
    I Am the Only Presence Here...

Until now I had had many experiences with this awareness, mainly one form at a time. Now I could feel this voice speak to me from everywhere as I drove along the interstate highway. And it was much more than a voice to be heard. It was a Presence to be felt...with...emanations from everywhere and everything.
I was lifted and exhalted...
I could feel the omnipresence...everywhere present...as I drove along the road...
I understood the experience...not as a teaching...

to be memorized…
to be remembered…
to be recited…
to be repeated…

I experienced it as the reality that it is…
In the experience, one's life does change…
The One life is felt…
And joy does come…

After this experience, I could allow awareness to see this reality in other places and at other times. I grew to realize the human staged events that were not yet open to this vast awareness. And I learned to be where I did feel that openness to be in that awareness.

Each of us can enter this spiritual universe that already IS…

Holy Sight and the Holy Mother

A deep and penetrating awareness came to me during the 1971 head on car collision. Through receptivity at the moment of impact, I was lifted into the Soul realm, seeing my life past, present and future through the eyes of joy. These experiences came not only though personal emergencies, but through planetary, global emergencies, such as the Chernobyl and 9-11 tragedies. No matter how the 'opening experiences of great upliftment,' came to me, I discovered that what seemed to be emergencies, turned out to be 'emergences.' They were openings to higher realms, thus were opportunities for 'breakthroughs' instead of 'breakdowns.' Fortunately for me, they were breakthroughs.

They turned out to be a form of holy visitation. I was introduced to and initiated into inner realities that I have never imagined. I could write a separate book about these epiphanies gifted to me in many forms. All the time, I was never asking for any of this. I did not even know the realms were there to ask for. I did not know that I could access the archetypes of wholeness. I did ask only for the realization of the Presence of God. That has been my burning desire.

Through the receptivity borne of meditation, I entered realms of the Holy Mother wearing many guises and scarves. I beheld her ecstatic faces and forms and actions. I came to know the Divine Feminine, the receptive principle, the yin of our being.

I beheld HER as Beauty, as shapeshifter in her vast ability to merge, as birther of new forms, as priestess warrior. I beheld her as the law of balance in the world of man and woman. She came often as the Dance of the One, that is the sacred dance of the Divine Two. She came as the Original One Woman, as Original Archetypal-SHE, as Infinity's Dance. She came to me as the Tribe of Cat (shared in another passage of this book) and she came to me often as owl. SHE revealed her fierce strength, will, determination that IS! SHE revealed unprecedented purity. SHE came in endless forms.

I have interpreted and translated the language of these inner illumined experiences into paintings, sculpture, poetry, sacred sounds and dance, and into soul sessions with the divine of others. To the human mind, these illumined emanations are as a foreign language. And we may each go within to have them translate, in the stillness of the Soul.

These transcendent experiences allowed me to behold the rapture and revelation of Oneness in many forms. I was lifted into the realm of the Blue Kachinas, Spider Woman (the world of all woman as One Woman), Changing Woman, White Buffalo Woman, Mother Mary, native chieftains and the Blue Star. I was lifted into the realm of Archetypal HE and SHE where I saw the procession of the ages and the emerging new world. I was lifted into the realm of the serpents, where hundreds of snakes entered my crown and feet and merged in my heart, where opened the fullness of the understanding of universal Love. I was lifted once into the realm where the sky entered my crown and the earth entered my feet. Earth and sky did merge in my heart and I was further lifted into a realm of Unspeakable purity.

In all of these experiences was the theme of Oneness. In all of them was the awareness of a love beyond human imaginings. And in all of them was a great revelation into the glory of the Mystical Marriage within, which can then be lived in man and woman who are attuned at those levels. In all of this, visions wove like illumined strands into the fabric of a new world, a new culture emerging from the law of balance, the law of love, the law of giving and equal regiving.

I am sharing some of these experiences now to share why I opened to work as a spiritual educator, as well as mystic artist, sculptress, poet, and ceremonialist of sounds and signings of the soul. Borne in me was the desire to inspire, catalyze and initiate transcendent remembering and awareness in others. I desired to share. We are all here to share fully of who we are and of the gifts that we do bring.

At one time, I was struggling for long months with a human emotional attachment to my oldest daughter. I had not even known that I had the attachment until life caused it to appear. When all my inner work did not help me, I surrendered to the mystical Presence at ever deeper levels. I finally admitted that I needed help. I realized that all of my efforts seemed to be useless and futile. In that deepened state of aspiration, I received a visitation. While shopping in a local store, I was overshadowed by Mother Mary, the Holy Mother. I was lifted out of ordinary human consciousness. Ecstasy filled my being. I witnessed all the people in the store from an illumined place, while paradoxically I could see their human sorrow and fear and could see how it was embedded in them because of beliefs about their finite sense of reality.

For the next year, I did one painting a month that was part of a Holy Mother series. I saw this divine countenance with many faces.
She is full of love and compassion and kindness.
She is the protector and guardian of life that has
    fierce and fiery faces and gestures and actions, as called for.
She is changing and moving.
She is knowing, in a simple and direct way.
She is the law of balance, lived.

I have come to know this Holy Mother as a Presence that is the mediator between the above and below, the within and without.

She is that which we touch as we open to this Presence…
She is that which we touch as we become receptive to It…
And…She…it is…who touches our lives as we come unto her Presence…
She…it is…who unveils and dissolves the finite, human sense of separation…
She…unveils herself as union…
She…exposes Her-self as One…

In the practice of Holy Sight, we do 'feel' the Presence in our self and other ones, other things and other places and even other times. In that, do we deepen our experience with the Holy Spirit, the Presence, the Holy Mother. Together…let us behold.

Holy Sight and Birthing

When I was almost complete with this book, it became clear to me that I needed to include this passage about Holy Sight and Birthing.

In 1970, I had a conventional and painful birthing in a hospital. My husband of the time did not want to be at the birth. I felt alone and isolated from life. I was not even allowed to spend the first nights with my new infant. It was an excruciating experience for me, as I could feel this precious new soul calling for me. And I could feel myself calling for her. The nurses delivered her to me before all the other babies in the morning and they picked her up for the nursery last in the evening, as they reported that she screamed the loudest for me. They wanted her out of the nursery. And so did I. This birth was all I knew. No options were offered in this Midwest town.

In 1974, I became pregnant again. I vowed never to repeat that first birthing experience and I was saddened that that was the first experience of life for my daughter. I was now living in California and the awareness around birthing was like living on another planet.

I began to read every book that I could on natural and home childbirth. I read of many types of birth, including water births. I decided that I wanted to experience the soul of birthing in a more universal sense. I wanted a conscious birth. I had no idea all that might mean, other than the stories I was reading.

One early morning at the local grocery store a block away from home, I was aware that the birth was about to begin. My intuition had grown strong from meditation. My oldest daughter sat with me for many hours of these meditations for 9 months. When I returned home, I called the midwife and the doctor and his wife, a nurse. I let them know that the birth was immediate. The doctor and nurse team who came to my home were there for the residue of fear in me left from the first birth. The midwife was there for my passage into a new birthing.

I had a 45 minute birth, which was painless, as long as I allowed the birth to be animated by sounds and movements of the soul that poured through me. The midwife encouraged my sounds, movements and positions that arose. The birth had its own life. I was witness of the birth. I beheld the birth as it happened through me.

As long as I continued the soul sounds that emerged, I felt connected to a cosmic sound ray, that made it a painless birth. And my physical body positioned itself from a place of inner knowing. I never needed to push. The birth simply unfolded through me.

Years later, in looking upon that mystical birth, I realize that in the nine months of reading, I was acquiring Holy Sight for birthing. I looked beyond, yet did not ignore, the practical and physical aspects. I did all of the earth plane preparations. I also did the soul preparation. In looking beyond, I experienced an ecstasy.

In Closing

Part of how this book came to be is that individuals coming to me for retreats and sessions began to say, "you must write a book about this work." Then one morning a phone call came in asking what I had been doing early that a.m. I said I had been meditating. The friend said that at that time she was shown an awareness of me, with a being standing over my shoulder. She said the being was helping me write a book.

As the months passed, the book just began coming on its own. The passages would just drop into my mind in the early predawns, driving on the freeways to work at the next city, sitting at the river's edge in Mount Shasta and while I was retreating in New Mexico.

May it serve to inspire, catalyze and initiate great remembering and awareness of the Oneness that we are.

Sacred Art of Mary Saint-Marie
Art-of-the-Soul

Mary Saint-Marie/Sheoekah is a mystical and visionary artist, poet, educator and ceremonial initiator of sacred sounds and signings of the soul.

Biography and education

Nature was the major childhood teacher of Mary Saint-Marie. Her formal university education included degrees in Education and English, after which she spent 8 years teaching high school and college English, Mythology and Communication. Soon after she was coordinator and script writer for public educational TV. Simultaneously, Mary studied Fine Arts at the University of Wisconsin. While teaching English at an Oregon college in 1971, Mary had a spontaneous soul merging experience followed shortly by a head-on car collision where she saw her "life via her Soul." This was the catalyst to be an artist and for a solo journey overland to Spain, Morocco, Italy, Greece, Crete, Turkey, Iran, Afghanistan, Pakistan, India and Kashmir where she absorbed the art, culture, heart and soul of those peoples. Upon her return to the US, Mary began her first art exhibitions and traveled to wilderness areas around the US for almost 2 years with her daughter, Kimberly. Much of that time was used to learn to meditate. At that time there were no visionary galleries, and Mary helped to pioneer the beginning of a strong focus on visionary art. Mary did this by creating exhibits in workshops, conferences, symposiums and seminars having to do with spiritual awakening. (Art resume is available.) Since 1974, Mary has lived with simplicity in a quiet mountain retreat in Mount Shasta, California. Currently, Mary is living between Mount Shasta and another mountain retreat, Taos, New Mexico.

Philosophy

Art-of-the-Soul is my soul's mystical expression of Oneness, my glimpse of Star-Stone Essence, what I playfully call Galactic

Shamanism...or the union of Earth and Sky...or more simply put...Love...

Mystical journeys into the inner realms of Light are the dwelling places of my multimedia paintings, sculpture and poetry. Each piece reflects and inspires the Soul's Remembering. It reveals Spirit Essence as it beckons from the 'once upon a non-time.'
It reveals the formless as form and the invisible as visible.

Transparent and subtle mergings reveal the Consciousness of Being in Oneness with Creator as Creation in my body of work. Shapeshifting becomes reality. I share inner experiences that unveil the precious earth body as the Temple Template of Infinity and that unveil the exaltation of Archetypal HE and SHE...The Sacred Two...as the One.

Sessions, Retreats, Workshops, Art Exhibits

Soul Remembering sessions (for individuals, by phone or in person)

Soul Remembering retreats (for individuals and groups)

The Holy Sight workshop (experiential work for groups)

Sounds and Signings of the Soul (individual and group initiations into sacred sound and movement/dance)

SHE...it is...who Remembers – Sacred Enactment of Ancient Remembering/multi-media presentation with art slides, dance, sacred sounds, dance and narration from book, *Galactic Shamanism*, by Mary Saint-Marie

Art-of-the-Soul (shown in Ancient Beauty Studio by appointment) Original paintings, giclee fine art reproductions and commissions available
Bronze sculpture available (bronze available from a "Serpentine Flight" series)

Recordings (inquire about purchase of recordings)
SHE...it is...who Remembers (narration/recording of *GALACTIC SHAMANISM)*
Return to Oneness (recording of a poetic odyssey into the Animal Realm)

EarthCare Global TV – request information on the vision of profound unification of global earth care

This book is published by:
Ancient Beauty Studio
P.O. Box 704
Mount Shasta, California 96067

Contact Information
www.marysaintmarie.com
marysaintmarie@snowcrest.net
Mary Saint-Marie
P.O. Box 704
Mt. Shasta, CA 96067
530-926-0720

About the Author

Mary Saint-Marie/Sheoekah, mystic artist/poet/sculptress, initiatress, spiritual educator and author of *GALACTIC SHAMANISM* and poetic odyssey, *Return to Oneness* (recording), has traveled extensively facilitating *Soul Remembering* retreats and sessions and THE HOLY SIGHT workshops. She presents Sacred Enactments of Ancient Remembering, multimedia presentations titled, *SHE ... it is ... who Remembers.*

Art-of-the-Soul by Mary Saint-Marie is mystical/shamanic/ inspirational and mirrors our Oneness with Creator/Creation. Mary's sacred and visionary paintings/work are in *One Source Sacred Journeys, Songs from the Edge of Everything* and *The Ways of Spirit.* Her art is collected nationally and internationally and has appeared on cards, calendars and magazines, such as *Quest*, and recently, *Anemone* (Japan). Mary has been pioneering art that reveals universal principles since 1972 in galleries, conferences, symposiums, expositions and workshops.

I am

in deep gratitude

Mary Saint-Marie

for the long years of listening

in the silence...

unwavering...

safekeeping the illuminated thread

that reminds us out of

the labyrinth

and finally Home.

LD

Printed in the United States
69522LVS00005BB/526-552